FACILITY OF RAJASTHAN

GAJANAND SINWAL

ISBN 979-888555717-7

i dedicated this book to my brother

Avjrfu Fvajny

Contents

Foreword

thanks for this

CHAPTER ONE

Bearded Collie

The legend of the Bearded Collie's origin is that the ancestors of what is today the Polish Lowland Sheepdog were abandoned on the shores of Scotland, and these dogs then bred with native herding dogs.[3] A variant on this story is that Kazimierz Grabski, a Polish merchant, reportedly traded a shipment of grain for sheep in Scotland in 1514 and brought six Polish Lowland Sheepdogs to move them. A Scottish shepherd was so impressed with the herding ability of the dogs that he traded several sheep for several dogs.[4] The Polish sheepdogs were bred with local Scottish dogs to produce the Bearded Collie.

It is generally agreed that Mrs. G. Olive Willison founded the modern Bearded Collie in 1944 with her brown bitch, Jeannie of Bothkennar.[5] Jeannie was supposedly a Shetland Sheepdog, but Mrs. Willison received a Bearded Collie by accident. She was so fascinated by the dog that she wanted to begin breeding, so she began searching for a dog for Jeannie. While walking along the beach, Mrs. Willison met a man who was emigrating from Scotland; she became the owner of his grey dog, David, who became Bailie of Bothkennar.

Bailie and Jeannie of Bothkennar are the founders of the modern breed; there are only a few other registrable blood lines, preserved in large part by the perseverance of Mr. Nicolas Broadbridge (Sallen) and Mrs. Betty Foster (Bredon). These are based on Turnbull's Blue—a Bearded Collie from pure working stock, registered in ISDS when ISDS still registered non-Border Collies. He sired three litters of registerable Bearded Collies.

The breed became popular during the last half of the 20th century—propelled, in part, by Potterdale Classic at Moonhill, a Bearded Collie who won Best in Show at Crufts in 1989. The Bearded Collie Club celebrated its Golden Jubilee in 2005. The bearded collie is also very good natured and is good as a family pet and a working dog and a show dog.

As pets[edit]

A Bearded Collie with a toy rope.

The Bearded Collie ranks 117 out of 175 breeds in popularity in the United States, according to the American Kennel Club's yearly breed ranking.[6] A Bearded Collie is best obtained from a reputable breeder or a dog rescue.[7][8] There are Beardie rescue associations, such as Beardie Collie Rescue[9] and "Rescue Me". These organisations attempt to place unwanted puppies and dogs into appropriate, loving homes. Most Bearded Collie breeders take great care in breeding, raising and placing their puppies.[10] Due to this, Bearded Collies are considered an "unspoiled" breed.[11]

Bearded Collies make excellent pets for those willing to accommodate their high energy level - they are very enthusiastic and have a bouncy nature. They also require regular grooming; weekly brushing is mandatory for keeping their long hair mat-free. Some Bearded Collie owners opt to keep their pets in a "puppy cut" haircut, which reduces (but does not eliminate) the need for brushing. Bearded Collies are an energetic breed, originally intended to work in the Scottish Highlands herding sheep; they also excel at treibball,[12] dog agility and Obedience trials. A loyal and family-friendly dog, the Beardie can add years of pet-ownership enjoyment to the home. They have keen problem-solving abilities, and are entertaining to watch.

In training, beardies can be independent, they will go from A to B but maybe not via the expected route. One of the most common problems for new Beardie owners is the breed's intelligence makes them prone to get quickly fed up if training gets too repetitive.

Working life[edit]

A Bearded Collie herding sheep.

The Bearded Collie is used to herd both sheep and cattle. It is essentially a working dog—bred to be hardy and reliable, able to stand up to the harshest conditions and the toughest sheep. The working Bearded Collie has become less common in the last few decades and risked dying out; however, thanks to the efforts of a few shepherds like Tom Muirhead and Peter Wood, the "working Beardie" has survived and is becoming more popular. It has been exported to Australia and the United States, and finds favour among those looking for an independent and intelligent sheepdog. The Working Bearded Collie Society's mission is to preserve the working abilities of non-registered working dogs from "bearded" ancestors. The website Shepherds with beardies has much valuable information on the small population of working Beardies.

The KC-registered Bearded Collie has fallen into disfavour with the shepherds of Wales, Scotland and elsewhere because of the show-breeding community's lack of interest in producing "hardy and reliable" animals; show-bred lines tend to develop excessive coats, in particular. However, in some countries (notably Sweden and the United States) herding programmes have been developed for the breed. The breed organisations in those countries actively encourage breeders to emphasise qualities other than appearance.

The Bearded Collie may have earned its nickname "bouncing Beardie" because the dogs would work in thick underbrush on hillsides; they would bounce to catch sight of the sheep. Beardies also have a characteristic way of facing a stubborn ewe, barking and bouncing on the forelegs. Whatever the reason, a typical Bearded Collie is an enthusiastic herding dog which requires structure and care; it moves stock with body, bark and bounce as required. Very few Beardies show "eye" when working; most are upright.

Herding instincts and tractability can be assessed in noncompetitive herding tests. Beardies exhibiting basic herding instincts can be trained to compete in herding trials.[13]

Health[edit]

A three-year-old Bearded Collie in Scotland.

The size of an average litter is seven pups.

Mortality[edit]

The median longevity (the age at which half of the population has died and half is still alive) of Bearded Collies from recent UK and USA/Canada surveys (the weighted average of all surveys) is 12.8 years; Beardies in the UK surveys lived longer (median ~13.4 years) than their USA/ Canada counterparts (median 12.0 years). Most purebred breeds have median longevities between 10 and 13 years and most breeds similar in size to Bearded Collies have median longevities between 11 and 13 years,[14] so the lifespan of Bearded Collies appears to be on the high end compared with other breeds (at least in the UK). Individual dogs may die much earlier or later than the median. In a 1996 USA/Canada survey, 32% of Beardies died (including accidental deaths) before the age of nine; however, 12% lived longer than 14 years.[15] The eldest of the 278 deceased dogs in the 2004 UK Kennel Club survey died at 19.5 years;[16] the age at death of the oldest dog in the USA/Canada survey was not reported.

Leading causes of death among Beardies in the UK are old age (26%), cancer (19%), cerebrovascular disease (9%), and chronic kidney failure (8%).[16] Leading causes of death among Beardies in the US and Canada are old age (18%), cancer (17%), kidney failure (8%), cerebrovascular disease (4%) and hypoadrenocorticism (4%).[15]

Morbidity[edit]

Bearded Collie owners in the UK reported that the most common health issues among living dogs were musculoskeletal—mostly arthritis and cruciate ligament rupture (CLR)—gastrointestinal (primarily colitis and diarrhea) and urologic diseases.[16] Beardie owners in the US and Canada reported that the most common health problems were hypothyroidism, cancer, hypoadrenocorticism (also known as Addison's disease), arthritis and skin problems. Morbidity in the two studies is not easily compared, however; the UK report grouped diseases, while the USA/Canada report ranked more specific conditions.

Further existing breed dispositions of the Bearded Collie include: Dermatological conditions, such as pemphigus foliaceous and black skin disease, follicular dysplasia, musculoskeletal conditions such as congenital elbow luxation, ocular conditions, such as corneal dystrophy, cataract and generalized progressive retinal atrophy (GPRA).[17]

Hypoadrenocorticism[edit]

Main article: Hypoadrenocorticism in dogs

Hypoadrenocorticism (also known as Addison's disease) is an inherited disease in Bearded Collies, although the mechanism of inheritance is not known.[18] It occurs when the adrenal cortex produces insufficient glucocorticoid and/or mineralocorticoid hormones. It affects approximately 2–3.4% of Bearded Collies in the USA/Canada,[15] and causes the death of at least 1% of Bearded Collies in the UK.[16] These are much higher percentages than for the general dog population (0.1%), and hypoadrenocorticism causes a disproportionate number of deaths among young dogs.[15] Early symptoms are vague and easily mistaken for other conditions. Symptoms include unexplained lethargy, frequent gastric disturbances, or an inability to tolerate stress. Untreated, hypoadrenocorticism can cause fatal sodium/potassium imbalances; with lifelong medication, most dogs can live a relatively normal life.

In popular culture[edit]

The role of Nana in the original production of the James Barrie play Peter Pan was performed by a Bearded Collie.[citation needed]

A Bearded Collie named Coal[19] featured in the 2006 film The Shaggy Dog starring Tim Allen.[20]

Ralphie, a Bearded Collie, appears in the 2009 film Hotel for Dogs.

CHAPTER TWO

life

All known life forms share fundamental molecular mechanisms, reflecting their common descent; based on these observations, hypotheses on the origin of life attempt to find a mechanism explaining the formation of a universal common ancestor, from simple organic molecules via pre-cellular life to protocells and metabolism. Models have been divided into "genes-first" and "metabolism-first" categories, but a recent trend is the emergence of hybrid models that combine both categories.[138]

There is no current scientific consensus as to how life originated. However, most accepted scientific models build on the Miller–Urey experiment and the work of Sidney Fox, which show that conditions on the primitive Earth favored chemical reactions that synthesize amino acids and other organic compounds from inorganic precursors,[139] and phospholipids spontaneously form lipid bilayers, the basic structure of a cell membrane.

Living organisms synthesize proteins, which are polymers of amino acids using instructions encoded by deoxyribonucleic acid (DNA). Protein synthesis entails intermediary ribonucleic acid (RNA) polymers. One possibility for how life began is that genes originated first, followed by proteins;[140] the alternative being that proteins came first and then genes.[141]

However, because genes and proteins are both required to produce the other, the problem of considering which came first is like that of the chicken or the egg. Most scientists have adopted the hypothesis that because of this, it is unlikely that genes and proteins arose independently.[142]

Therefore, a possibility, first suggested by Francis Crick,[143] is that the first life was based on RNA,[142] which has the DNA-like properties of information storage and the catalytic properties of some proteins. This is called the RNA world hypothesis, and it is supported by the observation that many of the most critical components of cells (those that evolve the slowest) are composed mostly or entirely of RNA. Also, many critical cofactors (ATP, Acetyl-CoA, NADH, etc.) are either nucleotides or substances clearly related to them. The catalytic properties of RNA had not yet been demonstrated when the hypothesis was first proposed,[144] but they were confirmed by Thomas Cech in 1986.[145]

One issue with the RNA world hypothesis is that synthesis of RNA from simple inorganic precursors is more difficult than for other organic molecules. One reason for this is that RNA precursors are very stable and react with each other very slowly under ambient conditions, and it has also been proposed that living organisms consisted of other molecules before RNA.[146] However, the successful synthesis of certain RNA molecules under the conditions that existed prior to life on Earth has been achieved by adding alternative precursors in a specified order with the precursor phosphate present throughout the reaction.[147] This study makes the RNA world hypothesis more plausible.[148]

Geological findings in 2013 showed that reactive phosphorus species (like phosphite) were in abundance in the ocean before 3.5 Ga, and that Schreibersite easily reacts with aqueous glycerol to generate phosphite and glycerol 3-phosphate.[149] It is hypothesized that Schreibersite-containing meteorites from the Late Heavy Bombardment could have provided early reduced phosphorus, which could react with prebiotic organic molecules to form phosphorylated biomolecules, like RNA.[149]

In 2009, experiments demonstrated Darwinian evolution of a two-component system of RNA enzymes (ribozymes) in vitro.[150] The work was performed in the laboratory of Gerald Joyce, who stated "This is the first example, outside of biology, of evolutionary adaptation in a molecular genetic system."[151]

Prebiotic compounds may have originated extraterrestrially. NASA findings in 2011, based on studies with meteorites found on Earth, suggest DNA and RNA components (adenine, guanine and related organic molecules) may be formed in outer space.[152][153][154][155]

In March 2015, NASA scientists reported that, for the first time, complex DNA and RNA organic compounds of life, including uracil, cytosine and thymine, have been formed in the laboratory under outer space conditions, using starting chemicals, such as pyrimidine, found in meteorites. Pyrimidine, like polycyclic aromatic hydrocarbons (PAHs), the most carbon-rich chemical found in the universe, may have been formed in red giants or in interstellar dust and gas clouds, according to the scientists.[156]

According to the panspermia hypothesis, microscopic life—distributed by meteoroids, asteroids and other small

Solar System bodies—may exist throughout the universe.[157][158]

Environmental conditions

Cyanobacteria dramatically changed the composition of life forms on Earth by leading to the near-extinction of oxygen-intolerant organisms.

The diversity of life on Earth is a result of the dynamic interplay between genetic opportunity, metabolic capability, environmental challenges,[159] and symbiosis.[160][161][162] For most of its existence, Earth's habitable environment has been dominated by microorganisms and subjected to their metabolism and evolution. As a consequence of these microbial activities, the physical-chemical environment on Earth has been changing on a geologic time scale, thereby affecting the path of evolution of subsequent life.[159] For example, the release of molecular oxygen by cyanobacteria as a by-product of photosynthesis induced global changes in the Earth's environment. Because oxygen was toxic to most life on Earth at the time, this posed novel evolutionary challenges, and ultimately resulted in the formation of Earth's major animal and plant species. This interplay between organisms and their environment is an inherent feature of living systems.[159]

Biosphere

Main article: Biosphere

The biosphere is the global sum of all ecosystems. It can also be termed as the zone of life on Earth, a closed system (apart from solar and cosmic radiation and heat from the interior of the Earth), and largely self-regulating.[163] By the most general biophysiological definition, the biosphere is the global ecological system integrating all living beings and their relationships, including their interaction with the elements of the lithosphere, geosphere, hydrosphere, and atmosphere.

Life forms live in every part of the Earth's biosphere, including soil, hot springs, inside rocks at least 19 km (12 mi) deep underground, the deepest parts of the ocean, and at least 64 km (40 mi) high in the atmosphere.[164][165][166] Under certain test conditions, life forms have been observed to thrive in the near-weightlessness of space[167][168] and to survive in the vacuum of outer space.[169][170] Life forms appear to thrive in the Mariana Trench, the deepest spot in the Earth's oceans.[171][172] Other researchers reported related studies that life forms thrive inside rocks up to 580 m (1,900 ft; 0.36 mi) below the sea floor under 2,590 m (8,500 ft; 1.61 mi) of ocean off the coast of the northwestern United States,[171][173] as well as 2,400 m (7,900 ft; 1.5 mi) beneath the seabed off Japan.[174] In August 2014, scientists confirmed the existence of life forms living 800 m (2,600 ft; 0.50 mi) below the ice of Antarctica.[175][176] According to one researcher, "You can find microbes everywhere—they're extremely adaptable to conditions, and survive wherever they are."[171]

The biosphere is postulated to have evolved, beginning with a process of biopoesis (life created naturally from non-living matter, such as simple organic compounds) or biogenesis (life created from living matter), at least some 3.5 billion years ago.[177][178] The earliest evidence for life on Earth includes biogenic graphite found in 3.7 billion-year-old metasedimentary rocks from Western Greenland[122] and microbial mat fossils found in 3.48 billion-year-old sandstone from Western Australia.[123][124] More recently, in 2015, "remains of biotic life" were found in 4.1 billion-year-old rocks in Western Australia.[114][115] In 2017, putative fossilized microorganisms (or microfossils) were announced to have been discovered in hydrothermal vent precipitates in the Nuvvuagittuq Belt of Quebec, Canada that were as old as 4.28 billion years, the oldest record of life on earth, suggesting "an almost instantaneous emergence of life" after ocean formation 4.4 billion years ago, and not long after the formation of the Earth 4.54 billion years ago.[1][2][3][4] According to biologist Stephen Blair Hedges, "If life arose relatively quickly on Earth ... then it could be common in the universe."[114]

In a general sense, biospheres are any closed, self-regulating systems containing ecosystems. This includes artificial biospheres such as Biosphere 2 and BIOS-3, and potentially ones on other planets or moons.[179]

Range of tolerance

Deinococcus radiodurans is an extremophile that can resist extremes of cold, dehydration, vacuum, acid, and radiation exposure.

DNA was first isolated by Friedrich Miescher in 1869.[193] Its molecular structure was identified by James Watson and Francis Crick in 1953, whose model-building efforts were guided by X-ray diffraction data acquired by Rosalind Franklin.[194]

ntists reported that 1 trillion species are estimated to be on Earth currently with only one-thousandth of one percent described.[133]

The original Linnaean system has been modified over time as follows:

Cells reproduce through a process of cell division in which the parent cell divides into two or more daughter cells. For prokaryotes, cell division occurs through a process of fission in which the DNA is replicated, then the two copies are attached to parts of the cell membrane. In eukaryotes, a more complex process of mitosis is followed. However, the end result is the same; the resulting cell copies are identical to each other and to the original cell (except for mutations), and both are capable of further division following an interphase period.[216]

Multicellular organisms may have first evolved through the formation of colonies of identical cells. These cells can form group organisms through cell adhesion. The individual members of a colony are capable of surviving on their own, whereas the members of a true multi-cellular organism have developed specializations, making them dependent on the remainder of the organism for survival. Such organisms are formed clonally or from a single germ cell that is capable of forming the various specialized cells that form the adult organism. This specialization allows multicellular organisms to exploit resources more efficiently than single cells.[217] In January 2016, scientists reported that, about 800 million years ago, a minor genetic change in a single molecule, called GK-PID, may have allowed organisms to go from a single cell organism to one of many cells.[218]

Cells have evolved methods to perceive and respond to their microenvironment, thereby enhancing their adaptability. Cell signaling coordinates cellular activities, and hence governs the basic functions of multicellular organisms. Signaling between cells can occur through direct cell contact using juxtacrine signalling, or indirectly through the exchange of agents as in the endocrine system. In more complex organisms, coordination of activities can occur through a dedicated nervous system.[219]

Extraterrestrial

Main articles: Extraterrestrial life, Astrobiology, and Astroecology

Though life is confirmed only on Earth, many think that extraterrestrial life is not only plausible, but probable or inevitable.[220][221] Other planets and moons in the Solar System and other planetary systems are being examined for evidence of having once supported simple life, and projects such as SETI are trying to detect radio transmissions from possible alien civilizations. Other locations within the Solar System that may host microbial life include the subsurface of Mars, the upper atmosphere of Venus,[222] and subsurface oceans on some of the moons of the giant planets.[223][224] Beyond the Solar System, the region around another main-sequence star that could support Earth-like life on an Earth-like planet is known as the habitable zone. The inner and outer radii of this zone vary with the luminosity of the star, as does the time interval during which the zone survives. Stars more massive than the Sun have a larger habitable zone, but remain on the Sun-like "main sequence" of stellar evolution for a shorter time interval. Small red dwarfs have the opposite problem, with a smaller habitable zone that is subject to higher levels of magnetic activity and the effects of tidal locking from close orbits. Hence, stars in the intermediate mass range such as the Sun may have a greater likelihood for Earth-like life to develop.[225] The location of the star within a galaxy may also affect the likelihood of life forming. Stars in regions with a greater abundance of heavier elements that can form planets, in combination with a low rate of potentially habitat-damaging supernova events, are predicted to have a higher probability of hosting planets with complex life.[226] The variables of the Drake equation are used to discuss the conditions in planetary systems where civilization is most likely to exist.[227] Use of the equation to predict the amount of extraterrestrial life, however, is difficult; because many of the variables are unknown, the equation functions as more of a mirror to what its user already thinks. As a result, the number of civilizations in the galaxy can be estimated as low as 9.1 x 10−13, suggesting a minimum value of 1, or as high as 15.6 million (0.156 x 109); for the calculations, see Drake equation.

A "Confidence of Life Detection" scale (CoLD) for reporting evidence of life beyond Earth has been proposed.[228][229]

Artificial

Main articles: Artificial life and Synthetic biology

Artificial life is the simulation of any aspect of life, as through computers, robotics, or biochemistry.[230] The study of artificial life imitates traditional biology by recreating some aspects of biological phenomena. Scientists study the logic of living systems by creating artificial environments—seeking to understand the complex information processing that defines such systems. While life is, by definition, alive, artificial life is generally referred to as data confined to a digital environment and existence.

Synthetic biology is a new area of biotechnology that combines science and biological engineering. The common goal is the design and construction of new biological functions and systems not found in nature. Synthetic biology includes the broad redefinition and expansion of biotechnology, with the ultimate goals of being able to design and build engineered biological systems that process information, manipulate chemicals, fabricate materials and structures, produce energy, provide food, and maintain and enhance human health and the environment.[231]

Death

Main article: Death

Animal corpses, like this African buffalo, are recycled by the ecosystem, providing energy and nutrients for living creatures

Death is the termination of all vital functions or life processes in an organism or cell.[232][233] It can occur as a result of an accident, violence, medical conditions, biological interaction, malnutrition, poisoning, senescence, or suicide. After death, the remains of an organism re-enter the biogeochemical cycle. Organisms may be consumed by a predator or a scavenger and leftover organic material may then be further decomposed by detritivores, organisms that recycle detritus, returning it to the environment for reuse in the food chain.

One of the challenges in defining death is in distinguishing it from life. Death would seem to refer to either the moment life ends, or when the state that follows life begins.[233] However, determining when death has occurred is difficult, as cessation of life functions is often not simultaneous across organ systems.[234] Such determination therefore requires drawing conceptual lines between life and death. This is problematic, however, because there is little consensus over how to define life. The nature of death has for millennia been a central concern of the world's religious traditions and of philosophical inquiry. Many religions maintain faith in either a kind of afterlife or reincarnation for the soul, or resurrection of the body at a later date.[citation needed]

Extinction

Main article: Extinction

Extinction is the process by which a group of taxa or species dies out, reducing biodiversity.[235] The moment of extinction is generally considered the death of the last individual of that species. Because a species' potential range may be very large, determining this moment is difficult, and is usually done retrospectively after a period of apparent absence. Species become extinct when they are no longer able to survive in changing habitat or against superior competition. In Earth's history, over 99% of all the species that have ever lived are extinct;[236][128][129][130] however, mass extinctions may have accelerated evolution by providing opportunities for new groups of organisms to diversify.[237]

CHAPTER THREE

India

India, officially the Republic of India (Hindi: Bhārat Gaṇarājya),[23] is a country in South Asia. It is the seventh-largest country by area, the second-most populous country, and the most populous democracy in the world. Bounded by the Indian Ocean on the south, the Arabian Sea on the southwest, and the Bay of Bengal on the southeast, it shares land borders with Pakistan to the west;[f] China, Nepal, and Bhutan to the north; and Bangladesh and Myanmar to the east. In the Indian Ocean, India is in the vicinity of Sri Lanka and the Maldives; its Andaman and Nicobar Islands share a maritime border with Thailand, Myanmar and Indonesia.

Modern humans arrived on the Indian subcontinent from Africa no later than 55,000 years ago.[24][25][26] Their long occupation, initially in varying forms of isolation as hunter-gatherers, has made the region highly diverse, second only to Africa in human genetic diversity.[27] Settled life emerged on the subcontinent in the western margins of the Indus river basin 9,000 years ago, evolving gradually into the Indus Valley Civilisation of the third millennium BCE.[28] By 1200 BCE, an archaic form of Sanskrit, an Indo-European language, had diffused into India from the northwest,[29][30] unfolding as the language of the Rigveda, and recording the dawning of Hinduism in India.[31] The Dravidian languages of India were supplanted in the northern and western regions.[32] By 400 BCE, stratification and exclusion by caste had emerged within Hinduism,[33] and Buddhism and Jainism had arisen, proclaiming social orders unlinked to heredity.[34] Early political consolidations gave rise to the loose-knit Maurya and Gupta Empires based in the Ganges Basin.[35] Their collective era was suffused with wide-ranging creativity,[36] but also marked by the declining status of women,[37] and the incorporation of untouchability into an organised system of belief.[g][38] In South India, the Middle kingdoms exported Dravidian-languages scripts and religious cultures to the kingdoms of Southeast Asia.[39]

In the early medieval era, Christianity, Islam, Judaism, and Zoroastrianism put down roots on India's southern and western coasts.[40] Muslim armies from Central Asia intermittently overran India's northern plains,[41] eventually establishing the Delhi Sultanate, and drawing northern India into the cosmopolitan networks of medieval Islam.[42] In the 15th century, the Vijayanagara Empire created a long-lasting composite Hindu culture in south India.[43] In the Punjab, Sikhism emerged, rejecting institutionalised religion.[44] The Mughal Empire, in 1526, ushered in two centuries of relative peace,[45] leaving a legacy of luminous architecture.[h][46] Gradually expanding rule of the British East India Company followed, turning India into a colonial economy, but also consolidating its sovereignty.[47] British Crown rule began in 1858. The rights promised to Indians were granted slowly,[48][49] but technological changes were introduced, and ideas of education, modernity and the public life took root.[50] A pioneering and influential nationalist movement emerged, which was noted for nonviolent resistance and became the major factor in ending British rule.[51] In 1947 the British Indian Empire was partitioned into two independent dominions, a Hindu-majority Dominion of India and a Muslim-majority Dominion of Pakistan, amid large-scale loss of life and an unprecedented migration.[52]

India has been a federal republic since 1950, governed in a democratic parliamentary system. It is a pluralistic, multilingual and multi-ethnic society. India's population grew from 361 million in 1951 to 1.211 billion in 2011.[53] During the same time, its nominal per capita income increased from US$64 annually to US$1,498, and its literacy rate from 16.6% to 74%. From being a comparatively destitute country in 1951,[54] India has become a fast-growing major economy and a hub for information technology services, with an expanding middle class.[55] It has a space programme which includes several planned or completed extraterrestrial missions. Indian movies, music, and spiritual teachings play an increasing role in global culture.[56] India has substantially reduced its rate of poverty, though at the cost of increasing economic inequality.[57] India is a nuclear-weapon state, which ranks high in military expenditure. It has disputes over Kashmir with its neighbours, Pakistan and China, unresolved since the mid-20th century.[58] Among the socio-economic challenges India faces are gender inequality, child malnutrition,[59] and rising levels of air pollution.[60] India's land is megadiverse, with four biodiversity hotspots.[61] Its forest cover comprises 21.7% of its area.[62] India's wildlife, which has traditionally been viewed with tolerance in India's culture

CHAPTER FOUR

Rajasthan

Rajasthan (/ˈrɑːdʒəstɑːn/; Hindustani pronunciation: [rɑːdʒəsˈt̪ʰɑːn] (listen); lit. 'Land of Kings')[8] is a state in northern India.[9][10][11] It covers 342,239 square kilometres (132,139 sq mi) or 10.4 percent of India's total geographical area. It is the largest Indian state by area and the seventh largest by population. It is on India's northwestern side, where it comprises most of the wide and inhospitable Thar Desert (also known as the Great Indian Desert) and shares a border with the Pakistani provinces of Punjab to the northwest and Sindh to the west, along the Sutlej-Indus River valley. It is bordered by five other Indian states: Punjab to the north; Haryana and Uttar Pradesh to the northeast; Madhya Pradesh to the southeast; and Gujarat to the southwest. Its geographical location is 23.3 to 30.12 North latitude and 69.30 to 78.17 East longitude, with the Tropic of Cancer passing through its southernmost tip.

Its major features include the ruins of the Indus Valley Civilisation at Kalibangan and Balathal, the Dilwara Temples, a Jain pilgrimage site at Rajasthan's only hill station, Mount Abu, in the ancient Aravalli mountain range and in eastern Rajasthan, the Keoladeo National Park of

Bharatpur, a World Heritage Site[12] known for its bird life. Rajasthan is also home to three national tiger reserves, the Ranthambore National Park in Sawai Madhopur, Sariska Tiger Reserve in Alwar and the Mukundra Hills Tiger Reserve in Kota.

The state was formed on 30 March 1949 when Rajputana – the name adopted by the British Raj for its dependencies in the region[13] – was merged into the Dominion of India. Its capital and largest city is Jaipur. Other important cities are Jodhpur, Kota, Bikaner, Ajmer, Bharatpur and Udaipur. The economy of Rajasthan is the seventh-largest state economy in India with ?10.20 lakh crore (US$140 billion) in gross domestic product and a per capita GDP of ?118,000 (US$1,600).[3] Rajasthan ranks 29th among Indian states in human development index.[5]

CHAPTER FIVE

Etymology Rajasthan

Etymology

Rajasthan literally means "The Land of Kings".[8] The oldest reference to Rajasthan is found in a stone inscription dated back to 625 CE.[14] The first printed mention of the name Rajasthan appears in the 1829 publication Annals and Antiquities of Rajasthan or the Central and Western Rajpoot States of India, while the earliest known record of Rajputana as a name for the region is in George Thomas's 1800 memoir Military Memories.[15] John Keay, in his book India: A History, stated that Rajputana was coined by the British in 1829, John Briggs, translating Ferishta's history of early Islamic India, used the phrase "Rajpoot (Rajput) princes" rather than "Indian princes".[16]

History

Main articles: History of Rajasthan and List of battles of Rajasthan

Ancient

Parts of what is now Rajasthan were partly part of the Vedic Civilisation and the Indus Valley Civilization. Kalibangan, in Hanumangarh district, was a major provincial capital of the Indus Valley Civilization.[17] Another archaeological excavation at the Balathal site in Udaipur district shows a settlement contemporary with the

Harrapan civilisation dating back to 3000–1500 BCE.

Stone Age tools dating from 5,000 to 200,000 years were found in Bundi and Bhilwara districts of the state.[18]

Matsya Kingdom of the Vedic civilisation of India is said to roughly corresponded to the former state of Jaipur in Rajasthan and included the whole of Alwar with portions of Bharatpur.[19][20] The capital of Matsya was at Viratanagar (modern Bairat), which is said to have been named after its founder king Virata.[21][need quotation to verify]

Bhargava[22] identifies the two districts of Jhunjhunu and Sikar and parts of Jaipur district along with Haryana districts of Mahendragarh and Rewari as part of Vedic state of Brahmavarta. Bhargava also locates the present day Sahibi River as the Vedic Drishadwati River, which along with Saraswati River formed the borders of the Vedic state of Brahmavarta.[23] Manu and Bhrigu narrated the Manusmriti to a congregation of seers in this area only. The ashrams of Vedic seers Bhrigu and his son Chayvan Rishi, for whom Chyawanprash was formulated, were near Dhosi Hill, part of which lies in Dhosi village of Jhunjhunu district of Rajasthan and part of which lies in Mahendragarh district of Haryana.[24]

The Western Kshatrapas (405–35 BCE), the Saka rulers of the western part of India, were successors to the Indo-Scythians and were contemporaneous with the Kushans, who ruled the northern part of the Indian subcontinent. The Indo-Scythians invaded the area of Ujjain and established the Saka era (with their calendar), marking the beginning of the long-lived Saka Western Satraps state.[25]

Classical

Gurjara-Pratihara

Ghateshwara Mahadeva temple at the Baroli Temple Complex. The temples were built between the 10th and 11th centuries CE by the Gurjara-Pratihara dynasty.

The Gurjaras ruled for many dynasties in this part of the country; the region was known as Gurjaratra.[26] Up to the 10th century CE, almost all of North India acknowledged the supremacy of the Gurjaras, with their seat of power at Kannauj.[27]

The Gurjara Pratihar Empire acted as a barrier for Arab invaders from the 8th to the 11th century. The chief accomplishment of the Gurjara-Pratihara Empire lies in its successful resistance to foreign invasions from the west, starting in the days of Junaid. Historian R. C. Majumdar says that this was openly acknowledged by the Arab writers. He further notes that historians of India have wondered at the slow progress of Muslim invaders in India, as compared with their rapid advance in other parts of the world. Now there seems little doubt that it was the power of the Gurjara Pratihara army that effectively barred the progress of the Arabs beyond the confines of Sindh, their only conquest for nearly 300 years.[28]

Medieval and Early Modern

Prithviraj Chauhan defeated the invading Muhammad Ghori in the First Battle of Tarain in 1191. In 1192 CE, Muhammad Ghori decisively defeated Prithviraj at the Second Battle of Tarain. After the defeat of Chauhan in 1192 CE, a part of Rajasthan came under Muslim rulers. The principal centers of their powers were Nagaur and Ajmer. Ranthambhore was also under their suzerainty. At the beginning of the 13th century, the most prominent and powerful state of Rajasthan was Mewar. The Rajputs resisted the Muslim incursions into India, although a number of Rajput kingdoms eventually became subservient to the Delhi Sultanate.

The Rajputs put up resistance to the Islamic invasions with their warfare and chivalry for centuries. The Rana's of Mewar led other kingdoms in its resistance to outside rule. Rana Hammir Singh, defeated the Tughlaq dynasty and recovered a large portion of Rajasthan. The indomitable Rana Kumbha defeated the Sultans of Malwa, Nagaur and Gujarat and made Mewar the most powerful Rajput Kingdom in India. The ambitious Rana Sanga united the various Rajput clans and fought against the foreign powers in India. Rana Sanga defeated the Afghan Lodi Empire of Delhi and crushed the Turkic Sultanates of Malwa and Gujarat. Rana Sanga then tried to create an Indian empire but was defeated by the first Mughal Emperor Babur at Khanua. The defeat was due to betrayal by the Tomar king Silhadi of Raisen. After Rana Sangas death there was no one who could check the rapid expansion of the Mughal Empire.[29][page needed]

Hem Chandra Vikramaditya, the Hindu Emperor,[30][31] was born in the village of Machheri in Alwar District in 1501. He won 22 battles against Afghans, from Punjab to Bengal including states of Ajmer and Alwar in Rajasthan, and defeated Akbar's forces twice, first at Agra and then at Delhi in 1556 at Battle of Delhi[32] before acceding to the throne of Delhi and establishing the "Hindu Raj" in North India, albeit for a short duration, from Purana Quila in Delhi. Hem Chandra was killed in the battlefield at Second Battle of Panipat fighting against Mughals on 5 November 1556.

Akbar shoots the Rajput commander Jaimal using a matchlock, during the Siege of Chittor (1567–1568).

During Akbar's reign most of the Rajput kings accepted Mughal suzerainty, but the rulers of Mewar (Rana Udai

Singh II) and Marwar (Rao Chandrasen Rathore) refused to have any form of alliance with the Mughals. To teach the Rajputs a lesson Akbar attacked Udai Singh and killed Rajput commander Jaimal of Chitor and the citizens of Mewar in large numbers. Akbar killed 20,000 – 25,000 unarmed citizens in Chittor on the grounds that they had actively helped in the resistance.[33]

Maharana Pratap took an oath to avenge the citizens of Chittor, he fought the Mughal empire till his death and liberated most of Mewar apart from Chittor itself. Maharana Pratap soon became the most celebrated warrior of Rajasthan and became famous all over India for his sporadic warfare and noble actions. According to Satish Chandra, "Rana Pratap's defiance of the mighty Mughal empire, almost alone and unaided by the other Rajput states, constitutes a glorious saga of Rajput valor and the spirit of self-sacrifice for cherished principles. Rana Pratap's methods of sporadic warfare was later elaborated further by Malik Ambar, the Deccani general, and by Shivaji".[34]

Rana Amar Singh I continued his ancestor's war against the Mughals under Jehangir, he repelled the Mughal armies at Dewar. Later an expedition was again sent under leadership of Prince Khurram, which caused much damage to life and property of Mewar. Many temples were destroyed, several villages were put on fire and women and children were captured and tortured to make Amar Singh accept surrender.[35]

During Aurangzeb's rule Rana Raj Singh I and Veer Durgadas Rathore were chief among those who defied the intolerant emperor of Delhi. They took advantage of the Aravalli hills and caused heavy damage to the Mughal armies that were trying to occupy Rajasthan.[36][37]

After Aurangzeb's death Bahadur Shah I tried to subjugate Rajasthan like his ancestors but his plan backfired when the three Rajput Raja's of Amber, Udaipur, and Jodhpur made a joint resistance to the Mughals. The Rajputs first expelled the commandants of Jodhpur and Bayana and recovered Amer by a night attack. They next killed Sayyid Hussain Khan Barha, the commandant of Mewat and many other Mughal officers. Bahadur Shah I, then in the Deccan was forced to patch up a truce with the Rajput Rajas.[38] The Jats, under Suraj Mal, overran the Mughal garrison at Agra and plundered the city taking with them the two great silver doors of the entrance of the famous Taj Mahal which were then melted down by Suraj Mal in 1763.[39]

Over the years, the Mughals began to have internal disputes which greatly distracted them at times. The Mughal Empire continued to weaken, and with the decline of the Mughal Empire in the late 18th century, Rajputana came under the influence of the Marathas. The Maratha Empire, which had replaced the Mughal Empire as the overlord of the subcontinent, was finally replaced by the British Empire in 1818.[40]

In the 19th century, the Rajput kingdoms were exhausted, they had been drained financially and in manpower after continuous wars and due to heavy tributes exacted by the Maratha Empire. To save their kingdoms from instability, rebellions and banditry the Rajput kings concluded treaties with the British in the early 19th century, accepting British suzerainty and control over their external affairs in return for internal autonomy.[41]

9 798885 557177

Printed by Libri Plureos GmbH in Hamburg,
Germany